ALI & ALI

The Deportation Hearings

Also by the Authors

By Marcus Youssef, Guillermo Verdecchia, and Camyar Chai
  *The Adventures of Ali & Ali and the aXes of Evil:
  A Divertimento for Warlords**

By Guillermo Verdecchia and Marcus Youssef
  *A Line in the Sand**

By Guillermo Verdecchia
  *Another Country / Bloom**
  *Citizen Suárez**
  *Fronteras Americanas: American Borders**
  Insomnia (with Daniel Brooks)
  The Noam Chomsky Lectures (with Daniel Brooks)*

By Marcus Youssef
  *Adrift**
  Everyone (Unmet Obligation)
  How Has My Love Affected You?
  Jabber
  Peter Panties (with Niall McNeil)
  Winners and Losers (with James Long)

* Published by Talonbooks

ALI & ALI

The Deportation Hearings

a play by

Camyar Chai
Guillermo Verdecchia
Marcus Youssef

Talonbooks

© 2013 by Camyar Chai, Guillermo Verdecchia, and Marcus Youssef

Talonbooks
P.O. Box 2076, Vancouver, British Columbia, Canada V6B 3S3
www.talonbooks.com

Typeset in Scala

Printed and bound in Canada on 100% post-consumer recycled paper
Cover design by Marijke Friesen
Cover illustrations by Chloë Filson

First printing: 2013

Talonbooks gratefully acknowledges the financial support of the Canada
Council for the Arts, the Government of Canada through the Canada Book
Fund, and the Province of British Columbia through the British Columbia
Arts Council and the Book Publishing Tax Credit.

All rights reserved. No part of this book may be reproduced, stored in a
retrieval system, or transmitted, in any form or by any means, without the
prior written consent of the publisher or a licence from the Canadian Copyright Licensing Agency (Access Copyright). For a copyright licence, visit
accesscopyright.ca or call toll free to 1-800-893-5777.

Rights to produce Ali & Ali: The Deportation Hearings, in whole or in part, in
any medium by any group, amateur or professional, are retained by the
authors. Interested persons are requested to apply to the authors care of
Talonbooks.

LIBRARY AND ARCHIVES CANADA CATALOGUING IN PUBLICATION

Chai, Camyar, author   Ali & Ali : the deportation hearings /
Camyar Chai, Guillermo Verdecchia, Marcus Youssef.

Follow up to: The adventures of Ali & Ali and the aXes of evil.
Issued in print and electronic formats. ISBN 978-0-88922-782-8 (pbk.). —
ISBN 978-0-88922-783-5 (epub)

        I. Verdecchia, Guillermo, author II. Youssef, Marcus, author
III. Title. IV. Title: Ali and Ali. V. Title: Adventures of Ali & Ali and the
aXes of evil.

PS8605.H332A55 2013   C812'.6   C2013-906384-6
                                          C2013-906385-4

Be Good
Share and Co-operate
Use Your Words Not Your Fists
Talk to Animals

– THE BOOK OF SAMMI
CHAPTER 12, VERSE 4

Production History

The outstanding success of *The Adventures of Ali & Ali and the aXes of Evil* in 2004 inspired this second Ali & Ali misadventure. *Ali & Ali: The Deportation Hearings* was produced under the title *Ali & Ali 7: Hey Brother, Can You Spare Some Hope and Change?* by Neworld Theatre and presented in association with Cahoots Theatre Company at The Cultch (Vancouver East Cultural Centre) from April 14 to 24, 2010, with the following cast and crew:

Ali Ababwa	Marcus Youssef
Ali Hakim	Camyar Chai
Hong Kong	Lee Raugi Yu
Sukhvinder Dhaliwal	Laara Sadiq

Directed by Guillermo Verdecchia

Designed by Rob Lewis and Jonathon Ryder

It was subsequently rewritten and retitled and then presented at Factory Theatre in Toronto, October 7 to 17, 2010, with the following cast and crew:

Ali Ababwa	Marcus Youssef
Ali Hakim	Guillermo Verdecchia
Hong Kong	Paul Sun Hyung Lee
Sukhvinder Dhaliwal	Anita Majumder

Directed by Guillermo Verdecchia with Soheil Parsa and Jivesh Parasram

Designed by Rob Lewis and Jonathon Ryder

Characters

ALI ABABWA
   stateless refugee from Agraba; a Copt

ALI HAKIM
   stateless refugee from Agraba; a Sammi

HONG KONG
   Ali & Ali's actor

SUKI (Sukhvinder Dhaliwal)
   RCMP constable

TOM BUTLER (pre-recorded cameo appearance)
   He was the manager in *Josie and the Pussycats* and
   the mayor in *The Killing*. YouTube him.

VOICE-OVER

Ladies and gentlemen, boys and girls, the rumours
are true. Those ambulant Agrabanians, Ali and Ali,
are back with a new show! Straight from Salim's
Falafel Shoppe, they're here, they're live, and this
time, they've hired a MONGOLIAN! Yes, the Emirs of
Entertainment, the Wallahs of Whacky are proud to
present *Yo Mama, Osbama (or How We Learned to Stop
Worrying and Love the Half-Black President)*.

> *PROJECTION (text)*
> Act 1, Scene 1

VOICE-OVER

Co-developed for six years through three workshops
and eight readings, in collaboration with Immigrant
Experience Theatre Company and Fresh Off the Boat
Performance Collective. Presented with the generous
support of Puppets Not Pain, Ali and Ali is proud to
present Scene 1 of *Yo Mama, Osbama:* "The Night
Everything Changed."

> *PROJECTION (text)*
> November 4, 2008.
> The Night Everything Changed

> *HONG KONG plays JASWINDER, the daughter.*
> *BINDI, the wife, is a bunraku[1] puppet, manipulated*

---

1. A form of traditional Japanese puppet theatre, founded in Osaka in 1684.
   Or so says Wikipedia.

I

by ALI ABABWA. JASWINDER watches TV. It's
U.S. election night. The sound of a CNN broadcast, then
a creaky door opening, wind blowing, and the door closing.

Enter ALI HAKIM as MOHANDES, brushing snow
off his shoulders and clutching a Tim Hortons cup.

MOHANDES
Bad news, nah. I have been laid off my occupation at
chicken processor plant.

BINDI
Oh, Mohandes. What will we do?

MOHANDES
Make me some vindaloo.

BINDI
We have no money for ingredients.

MOHANDES
Oh, Lakshmi, why is the global economy melting
down? I have Ph.D. in nuclear physics but here am I,
a pauper in a cold country.

JASWINDER
Dad. Come and watch this.

MOHANDES
What is it, Jasmine?

JASWINDER
Barack Hussein Osbama.

MOHANDES
Oh yes, the black fellow. (*makes monkey noises*)

JASWINDER

Don't do that, Dad. I think he's going to become
president of the United States.

MOHANDES

Oh sure. And I am going to become president of the
Canadian Atomic Energy Institute-nah.

BINDI

I believe you will, Mohandes. One day.

MOHANDES

I apologize, my daughter, to make such a racist
comment. It is because of the pain I am feeling.
Bindi, my wife, I am sorry to be such a failure.
You deserve better. You should have married
Nehru Netanyahu, the carpet king of Bangalore.

BINDI

I married you, Mohandes, and you are not a failure.
As my grandmother used to say, "Life is like a box of
gulab jamun. You never know when –"

JASWINDER

The results from Florida are coming in!

*They gather around the TV. They are transfixed by the
miracle unfolding.*

MOHANDES, BINDI & JASWINDER

By the blue epidermis of Krishna ...

JASWINDER

It's really happening. This is history. This is a whole
new era of hope and change.

MOHANDES
I'm not convinced. Is it legal for a black man to be president?

JASWINDER
Don't you see? *Everything's different now.*

The phone rings.

MOHANDES
If that's any boys sniffing around to take her to Club Shambar, you tell them Jaswinder is studying.

BINDI
It's for you, Mohandes. It's the Canadian Atomic Energy Institute-nah. They want you to be their president.

MOHANDES
Oh ... Bindi.

JASWINDER
I love you, Dad.

MOHANDES
I love you too, Jaswinder.

BINDI
Everything really is different now.

Music. Lights. Applause. Maybe.

ALI HAKIM
(*to audience*) Thank you.

ALI ABABWA
(*to audience*) Thank you, ladies and gentlemen, for coming to Factory Theatre Studio Shithole.[2]

ALI HAKIM
Allow us to introduce ourselves.

ALI ABABWA
I am Ali Ababwa.

ALI HAKIM
And I – Allah be praised – am not.

ALI ABABWA
We are stateless refugees

ALI HAKIM
from Agraba.

ALI ABABWA & ALI HAKIM
Here are our papers.

ALI ABABWA
We came to the United States of Canada six years ago to do our theatre-play *World Dreaming Together.*

ALI HAKIM
It was a very dark time.

PROJECTION (image)
George W. Bush burning. Like a bush

---

2. In this site-specific reference, we were quite mean about the Factory Theatre Studio. (It is basically a shithole, but … perhaps it was the rat in the dressing room that got us going.) In Vancouver, at The Cultch, we said, "Thank you for coming to Gentrified Vancouver East Church Basement."

ALI ABABWA
But now things are different.

ALI HAKIM
Where once the Devil himself led the West into two
wars and a global clash of civilizations

ALI ABABWA
now a well-spoken, Nobel Prize–winning black man
leads the West into two wars and a clash of
civilizations. But he's a Democrat! To those who doubt
the transformational power of the pan-African
socialist president's reign

ALI HAKIM
we say: Shut the fuck up.

ALI ABABWA
You have to admit, the mulatto fellow ...

PROJECTION (image)
Obama shirtless

They ululate excitedly.

... is pretty sexy. And let's face it, he's about as good as
we're ever going to get.

ALI HAKIM
Sure Guantanamo's still open.

ALI ABABWA
And thousands of people have been blown to bits by
drone attacks.

ALI HAKIM
And the U.S. is spying on –

ALI ABABWA
But have you heard him speak?

ALI HAKIM
So eloquent

ALI ABABWA
and heartfelt – and that chocolatey skin! Somehow it's better hearing all that stuff from a black man.

ALI HAKIM
So in tribute to the president of your great country

ALI ABABWA
we are proud to present our brand new theatre-play

ALI HAKIM
Yo Mama, Osbama (or

ALI ABABWA
How We Learned to Stop Worrying and Love the Half-Black President)

ALI HAKIM
co-starring one of Canada's best-known yellow actors

ALI ABABWA & ALI HAKIM
Hong Kong Lee.

HONG KONG
(*aside to ALI ABABWA and ALI HAKIM*) My name's Sun Hyung –

ALI HAKIM
  (*aside to HONG KONG*) Shut up, fool. You have no
  lines here.

HONG KONG
  (*to ALI ABABWA and ALI HAKIM*) And Obama's not –

ALI ABABWA
  Let us sing.

ALI HAKIM, ALI ABABWA & HONG KONG
  (*singing*)
    A new new world
    A really new new new day
    When you hope and change
    Yes, we can!
    Please please please please
    Let it be a whole new world with you
    Osbama

ALI ABABWA
  (*to audience*) Oh, the night President Osbama was
  elected, remember?

ALI HAKIM
  You went crazy.

ALI ABABWA
  We all did. Don't you just love it when black people
  are happy? We watched through window of restaurant
  on College, our noses pressed against the glass.

ALI HAKIM
  (*to ALI ABABWA*) No. We were with Salim at
  Falafel Shoppe.

ALI ABABWA
(to ALI HAKIM) No, we were outside restaurant.

ALI HAKIM
No. We were with Salim. Meeting at Falafel Shoppe,
remember?

ALI ABABWA
(to audience) The MODERATE Falafel Shoppe, ladies
and gentlemen. For more information about Ali & Ali

ALI HAKIM
and the 1001 varieties of bubble tea available at
Salim's Friendly Arabian Falafel Shoppe

ALI ABABWA
please visit our website: www

ALI HAKIM ululates.

ALI ABABWA
dot com. You can sign up for tweets too.

HONG KONG
(to ALI HAKIM) Mr. Hakim, seriously –

ALI HAKIM
(to HONG KONG) Do you mind?

HONG KONG
I'm sorry, but I really need to –

ALI HAKIM
This is how it works in Mongolia? The extras interrupt
whenever they please?

9

HONG KONG
Obama isn't Canada's president. We have our own
prime minister. Stephen Harper.

*They look at each other. HONG KONG motions to
control booth.*

PROJECTION (image)
*Prime Minister Stephen Harper looking friendly and
holding a kitten*

ALI HAKIM
You are mistaken, my little yellow friend. This is
manager of Tim Hortons on 400 near Barrie.

HONG KONG
No, it's not. That's Stephen Harper. The prime minister
of Canada.

ALI ABABWA
(*to audience*) No.

ALI HAKIM
Mr. Robocall?

ALI ABABWA
The guy who muzzles diplomats and scientists?

ALI HAKIM
Allows torture of Afghan detainees?

ALI ABABWA
Picks up the tab for all Mike Duffy's cheeseburgers?

ALI HAKIM
Wants to build prisons for criminals who don't exist?

ALI ABABWA
But he's holding a kitten. Is hard to believe he could
be so cruel.

ALI HAKIM
Hong Kong, ladies and gentlemen, we know this is
prime minister of Canada.

HONG KONG
Oh. A joke.

ALI HAKIM
Yes, fool!

HONG KONG
I thought you were serious. Like when Boltar mistakes
that leader of the Jingoes for the Moutardian Prince.

*HONG KONG exits. A beat while audience wonders
what he could possibly be talking about.*

ALI HAKIM
Back to show.

ALI ABABWA
While some from the Middle East like to blame the –

*HONG KONG appears, holding a phone; gestures to
ALI ABABWA.*

ALI HAKIM
What now?!

HONG KONG
It's the manager from Quickie Cash. He says he
wants his money.

ALI HAKIM
    QUICKIE CASH, Ali Ababwa?

ALI ABABWA
    Offer him a sponsorship.

HONG KONG
    He sounds really angry.

ALI ABABWA
    Talk to him in Japanese.

HONG KONG
    I don't speak Japanese.

ALI HAKIM
    Race traitor /

ALI ABABWA
    (*overlapping with ALI HAKIM*) / Give me that.
    (*takes the phone*) *Ich bin ein keine englishen speacken.*
    Eine kleine nachtmusik!

    ALI ABABWA hands the phone back to HONG KONG.

ALI ABABWA
    How hard was that? My apologies, Ali Hakim.

ALI HAKIM
    Quickie Cash, Ali Ababwa, is haram. Is usury, and
    (*to audience*) illegal in many Muslim countries, ladies
    and gentlemen.

ALI ABABWA
    (*to audience*) As we were saying, some from the
    Middle East like to blame the West for all their problems.

ALI HAKIM
They whine about colonialism

ALI ABABWA
orientalism

ALI HAKIM
the oil economy ...

ALI ABABWA
Still others complain about how they are treated once
they come to the West

ALI HAKIM
not being able to put a mosque in Manhattan or
Tennessee

ALI ABABWA
being racially profiled

ALI HAKIM
detained without charges

ALI ABABWA
deported to torture.

ALI HAKIM
But we know better.

ALI ABABWA
We have learned from your blogosphere that
Middle Easterners are a vicious, primitive people

ALI HAKIM
and *that* is why bad things are always happening to us.

ALI ABABWA

Fortunately, there are creative tools available which enable us to learn from you and your enlightened and multicultural example.

ALI HAKIM

In the tradition of the great master of Theatre for Social Action, Septembro Boali, we are proud to present to you Scene 2 of *Yo Mama, Osbama*.

> PROJECTION (image)
> A poster for Hamza and the Veil: A Dramatic Interception

ALI ABABWA

Hamza and the Veil: A Dramatic Interception. You will now witness a scene drawn from real-life stories of primitive behaviour shared with us at the Agrabanian Cultural Centre for Culture

ALI HAKIM

and Taxis.

ALI ABABWA

Then, the actors will perform the scene a second time, but this time, if any of you see a way to change the outcome, and prevent the behaviour from happening, you must raise your hand, say stop, and step into the role of one of the characters in the scene. In this way, we can learn from you. Don't worry, the actors are highly trained. Warn ... and curtain!

> *ALI HAKIM plays the oppressive MIDDLE EASTERN FATHER; HONG KONG plays HAMZA, the daughter[3] (caught between two cultures).*

---

3. In some remote parts of Agraba, some girls are sometimes named Hamza.

MIDDLE EASTERN FATHER
Hamza. It's about time you came home.

HAMZA
I'm sorry, Daddy. I was busy at the mosque.

MIDDLE EASTERN FATHER
Are you telling me the truth?

HAMZA
Of course, Daddy.

MIDDLE EASTERN FATHER
Then why did Akbar see you dancing at Club Shambar
with no veil on?!

HAMZA rips off her veil.

HAMZA
Fuck you, Daddy. I'm tired of your feudal, patrio-
Islamist, gender-policing ways. My tits are mine and
I'll show them to whomever I want.

MIDDLE EASTERN FATHER
Al-Mutah!

He slaps her.

ALI ABABWA
Stop! Great.

HONG KONG
(*clutching his face*) This is why we need a fight director.

ALI ABABWA
Is everybody okay?

ALI HAKIM
(*clutching his hand*) His face is very sharp!

ALI ABABWA
It's very intense, I know. Now we will repeat the
scene, this time looking for an audience member to
intercept and teach us how to change this all-too-
familiar, oppressive, culturally determined behaviour.
Warn ... and curtain.

The scene begins again.

MIDDLE EASTERN FATHER
Hamza. It's about time you came home.

HAMZA
I'm sorry, Daddy. I was busy at the mosque.

MIDDLE EASTERN FATHER
Are you telling me the truth?

HAMZA
Of course, Daddy.

*SUKI enters from the lobby. She wears full RCMP dress
uniform.*

SUKI
(*from the audience*) Excuse me.

ALI HAKIM & HONG KONG
Shhhhh!

ALI ABABWA
An interception! Excellent.

ALI HAKIM & HONG KONG
Oh.

ALI ABABWA
(*to ALI HAKIM and HONG KONG*) Hold.
(*to audience*) Who was it that raised their hand?

SUKI
(*to ALI ABABWA*) Me. (*to audience*) My apologies,
ladies and gentlemen.

ALI ABABWA
No need to apologize.

> *SUKI approaches the stage wearing her red serge
> uniform.*

ALI ABABWA
(*as she comes onstage*) I like your jacket by the way.
It must be traditional.

HONG KONG
Guys, she's really RCMP.

ALI ABABWA & ALI HAKIM
(*dismissively*) Of course. Yes, yes. For sure.

ALI ABABWA
(*to SUKI*) You have an idea about how to transform
the scene's outcome?

SUKI
I need you to stop.

ALI ABABWA
Go with your first impulse. But in your improvisation
you might find it useful to consider the postcolonial
tendency for the use of the veil to reflect a somewhat
feminist reclamation of traditional values in the face
of Western political and cultural hegemony.

SUKI
Gentlemen –

ALI HAKIM
Also you might keep in mind while improvising that
for many in the West the veil has become a synecdoche
of the monstrous Muslim Other.

HONG KONG
Actually, I think it's really important to recognize that
wearing the veil is often a very personal decision and
not about patriarchal –

They have crowded around her.

SUKI
I need you to take a step back.

ALI ABABWA
Sure.

They step back.

ALI ABABWA
Who would you like to replace?

SUKI
No –

ALI HAKIM
The daughter!

ALI ABABWA
Of course. Hamza. (*to SUKI*) You can just mime
lifting your shirt.

SUKI
I don't think any of us wants a scene here.

ALI HAKIM
Of course we do. That's the whole point.
(*to ALI ABABWA*) Philistine.

ALI ABABWA
We'll take it from, "Are you telling me the truth?"

ALI HAKIM
(*to SUKI*) Madam. No Bollywood.

ALI ABABWA
Warn and ... curtain.

MIDDLE EASTERN FATHER
Are you telling me the truth?

SUKI
Are you Mr. Ali –

MIDDLE EASTERN FATHER
(*bad stage whisper*) Of course, Daddy. I always tell the
truth.

SUKI
You are Messieurs Ali Ababwa and Ali Hakim.

MIDDLE EASTERN FATHER
AH!

ALI ABABWA
You must stay "in character," madam.

SUKI
I'm not a character.

ALI ABABWA
You are the daughter, Hamza. Ali Hakim is the father.

SUKI
No, I'm not doing that.

ALI ABABWA
It's not easy, we know. Don't be nervous.
The audience is on your side.

MIDDLE EASTERN FATHER
Why did Akbar see you dancing at Club Shambar?

SUKI
Okay. Uh, maybe you can answer some questions for
me, "Dad."

ALI ABABWA
Good, that's it!

SUKI
Do you know a cleric by the name of Nasr Al-Said?

MIDDLE EASTERN FATHER
Al-Said?

SUKI
Didn't he speak at the Al-Jihad mosque?

MIDDLE EASTERN FATHER
... Maybe. I don't remember. Uh, Al-*Jihad* mosque?

SUKI
Some of my "friends" say bad people hang out at that
mosque.

MIDDLE EASTERN FATHER
Your friends are whores!

SUKI
Really? How did you get into Canada, Dad?

MIDDLE EASTERN FATHER
No, I don't. I mean ... What about Club Shambar?

SUKI
Okay then, can you tell me about your relationship to
the APF?

MIDDLE EASTERN FATHER
What are you talking? APF?

SUKI
The Agrabanian People's Front.

MIDDLE EASTERN FATHER
...

ALI ABABWA
And scene!

SUKI

You are familiar with the APF.

ALI HAKIM

(*to ALI ABABWA*) I tell you this experimental shit doesn't work.

ALI ABABWA

(*to ALI HAKIM*) She didn't do it right. (*to SUKI*) You, sit down.

SUKI

Wait –

ALI ABABWA

(*to audience*) Big hand for our interceptor.

SUKI

No, I'm just getting started –

ALI HAKIM

(*to SUKI*) Madam, you are disrupting the theatre-play.

ALI ABABWA

Hong Kong! We need security!

ALI HAKIM

Get her out of here.

SUKI

I'm sorry, everyone, but not everything in this little skit is what it seems. I'm with the RCMP.

ALI HAKIM

Refugee Council Media Program?

SUKI

Royal Canadian Mounted Police. I'm stopping this
show.

ALI HAKIM

Stop the show?!

ALI ABABWA

(*aside to ALI HAKIM*) Shhh ... Taser ...

SUKI

Let's just say the curtain has come down.

ALI ABABWA

Please, kind lady, I promise soon I will be able to
reimburse munificent Quickie Cash loan
organization.

SUKI

Quickie Cash?

ALI ABABWA

... yes ... Quickie Cash Payday Loan. I failed to read the
fine print of my loan agreement. The interest rates are
quite a bit higher than one might reasonably expect
and so I find myself –

SUKI

I'm here on behalf of Immigration Canada.

ALI HAKIM

Immigration?

SUKI

That's right, and the Ministry of Citizenship and
Immigration has –

ALI ABABWA
Citizenship?

ALI ABABWA goes into hysterical joy.

Oh now I understand. You are confirming our
identities! The end of our wanderings, Ali Hakim,
has come! At last!

ALI HAKIM
It has?

ALI ABABWA
Hong Kong! Bring the ceremonial tapas! And the
martinis!

ALI HAKIM
Martinis?! *(runs off to help)*

SUKI
Sir –

ALI ABABWA
Please, dark-eyed deceptive messenger, allow me to
kiss your sweet face!

ALI ABABWA attempts to kiss SUKI.

SUKI
Don't kiss my face. *(stops him with a certified RCMP
empty-hand combat move)* You are exhibiting non-
compliant behaviours, sir. If you don't cease and
desist, I'll charge you with obstruction.

ALI ABABWA
(on his knees in a submission hold) You are quite strong.

HONG KONG returns with pastries and martinis.

HONG KONG
SNACKS!

ALI ABABWA
Please, enjoy an Agrabanian pastry. Shazzam
Hussein! And martinis for everyone!

HONG KONG offers SUKI a martini. She hesitates.

ALI HAKIM
It's made with genuine Agrabanian turnip vodka

SUKI
I'm on duty. Do you have a licence to serve alcohol in
a live-performance venue?

*HONG KONG shows her their licence. HONG KONG
distributes drinks and snacks to the audience.*

ALI ABABWA
It has been many difficult years since we fled the
country of our birth, Ali Hakim and I. May you never
know the sorrow and fear of the person with no
home. Allow me to detail the events that have led to
this glorious day in which we become citizens of your
magnificent coun– /

ALI HAKIM
(*overlapping with ALI ABABWA*) / CITIZENS? I am a
citizen of Agraba, Ali Ababwa. As are you.

ALI ABABWA
Our citizenship has arrived, Ali Hakim!

SUKI

Okay, that's enough.

ALI ABABWA

Don't worry, we are ready: John A. Macdonald. Ten
provinces, three territories. Nunavut. Boom Boom
Geoffrion –

SUKI

That's very impressive but –

ALI ABABWA

Residential schools, and I too am deeply sorry.
Air India, 1985, though I feel a bit self-conscious
saying that to you. And ... this year it's the Leafs
for sure.

SUKI

This is not a citizenship test! I'm from the Royal
Canadian Mounted Police. I am investigating you
under PEIU.

ALI HAKIM

PEIU? [peee-you]

SUKI

(*pronouncing it with a slightly Gallic accent*) PEIU.
The Provision for the Expulsion of Immigrant
Undesirables Act. Immigration minister Jason
Kenney passed it last year, as part of the budget.
They're passing it again this year. Just 'cause they
like it so much.

ALI HAKIM
     By Sammy, I tell you, Ali Ababwa, this is the secret
     police! (*turns to HONG KONG*) Why didn't you warn
     us she was a police?!

ALI ABABWA
     What have you done?

ALI HAKIM
     Me? It is you who is indebted to idolatrous
     moneylenders! Madam, we are in the middle of a
     performance. Perhaps you could leave us a card?

HONG KONG
     Can you be any more specific about these, uh …
     suspicions?

SUKI
     No. I can tell you that under PEIU, I am empowered
     by Her Majesty's Parliament to act as judge,
     prosecutor, stenographer, and – if necessary –
     marshal on designated immigration charter flights. If
     the court finds it necessary, you'll be deported to your
     country of origin.

HONG KONG
     Ma'am, if I may – there are no flights to Agraba. It's a
     war zone.

SUKI
     (*checking manual*) I think in that case you'll be sent
     to … Axerbijanistan.

     SUKI begins to set up her "courtroom."

ALI HAKIM
Axerbijanistan ...?

ALI ABABWA
But, madam, we all know the Axerbijanistanis are not exactly welcoming to Agrabanian deportees.

HONG KONG
There's a long and detailed archive of abuses and violations. The International Criminal Court recently ruled –

SUKI's phone rings.

SUKI
(*ignoring phone*) Canada's Conservative government also has a provision for indefinite detention.

HONG KONG
It's just like the security certificate detainees.

ALI ABABWA
Is that legal?

HONG KONG
It is on Planet 9. Because of the Fangorian uprising.

ALI ABABWA
That's a comic book.

HONG KONG
Graphic novel. And you can pooh-pooh speculative fiction all you want, but I'd say Exodus Chronicles is a pretty powerful allegory for a lot of things going on in our world right now.

ALI ABABWA
Shhh! I respect your cultural practices.

HONG KONG
As Boltar says, "Ignore us at your peril."

SUKI answers her phone.

SUKI
Mom, what's going on? I can't. The babysitter's name
is Brittany. I don't know where she is. Mom ... Mom ...
Mom.

ALI HAKIM
I'm not going back to Axerbijanistan, Ali Ababwa,
Never, I would sooner die.

ALI ABABWA
Don't talk like that, Ali Hakim. Only God knows
where the desert ends.

ALI HAKIM
Bribe her.

HONG KONG
No, that's not a good idea.

SUKI
(*on phone*) She's a perfectly nice girl and Jiv loves her.

ALI ABABWA
I only have a loonie.

ALI HAKIM
Take a collection.

HONG KONG
A legal defence fund.

SUKI

(*on phone*) Oh for fuck's sake, I'm in the middle of a hearing.

ALI ABABWA

(*to audience*) Ladies and gentlemen, apologies for breaching the divide. We are wondering if any of you would care to donate to the SPCA: Society for the Prevention of Cruelty to Agrabanians.

SUKI

(*hanging up phone; to audience*) Sorry. Personal matter.

Beat.

This theatre is now a court of law. Do you understand?

ALI HAKIM

Please, Mrs. Singh. Agrabanians invented jurisprudence.

SUKI

My name is Sukvinder Dhaliwal. You should refer to me as Constable.

ALI ABABWA & ALI HAKIM
Yes, sir.

SUKI

(*to audience*) As part of PEIU's Enforced Transparency Provision, I have to ask you all to stay. I apologize if you're inconvenienced but you're all witnesses. Please raise your right hand. Everyone, please. (*to ALI ABABWA and ALI HAKIM*) Let's have some light for the audience.

ALI ABABWA
Sure. (*addresses the control booth*) Ah, Akbar.

House lights come on.

SUKI
Repeat after me. (*reading from manual*) I solemnly swear ... to keep the content of these proceedings secret ... now and forever more ... So help me God ... or Whatever. Okay, good. Shit. Hang on.

She starts texting.

HONG KONG
What are you doing?

SUKI
I have to tweet. It's a social media initiative, to demonstrate transparency and appeal to a younger demographic. It's part of something they're calling Today's RCMP. You could follow me. If you want.

HONG KONG takes out his iPhone.

SUKI
I'm @SukidRCMP.

Pause while HONG KONG enters SUKI's Twitter name on his iPhone.

SUKI
Anyway.

PROJECTION (*image*)
Three-page document with key phrases blacked out

SUKI

(*reading*) "As prima facie evidence, the Crown
introduces the following: that you"

SUKI pauses for redaction.

"and further that you entered into"

Pause for redaction.

"and on January twenty-third, were"

Pause for redaction.

"who is known to"

Pause for redaction.

"as a"

Pause for redaction.

"Furthermore"

Pause.

"is"

Pause.

"to have been ..."

Pause.

How do you respond?

ALI HAKIM

It is hard to know what to say.

SUKI
Sensitive portions of the evidence against you have
been blacked out for reasons of national security.

HONG KONG
It is just like the security certificate detainees.

ALI ABABWA
This is not your Exodus Chronicles.

SUKI
Can I see your papers?

HONG KONG
Show her.

ALI HAKIM submits his "papers."

SUKI
This isn't a passport. It's a coupon for 10 percent off
at United Furniture Warehouse.

ALI HAKIM
Do you want it?

ALI ABABWA
Don't bother, it's expired.

SUKI
Mr. Ababwa?

ALI ABABWA
Yes, madam.

He produces his papers.

SUKI
This is a UN transit pass.

ALI ABABWA
Was very difficult to get.

SUKI
This is not a passport.

ALI ABABWA
They were lost in the war.

HONG KONG
As you know, ma'am, Agraba is in the midst of a decades-long conflict that has claimed many many lives.

SUKI
I see.

HONG KONG
You know that, right?

SUKI
I'm – generally aware.

HONG KONG
Generally?

SUKI
I don't think it's reasonable or realistic to expect any of us to be up to date on the details of every little conflict in every little corner of the globe. Do you?

HONG KONG
Well, actually ...

SUKI
My ex-husband, his family's from Sri Lanka, and I can't even keep track of the stuff going on over there. Tiger this, Sinhalese that.

ALI HAKIM
Oh sure.

ALI ABABWA
Those Tamil guys are crazy.

HONG KONG
Right, well. Just to let you know, in Agraba there's nothing resembling what we might consider a functioning government. These two fled in the wake of a major outbreak of violence. Mr. Ababwa is a minority Christian, and was subject to serious reprisals –

SUKI
Are you their lawyer?

HONG KONG
I could be.

ALI ABABWA
No, he's our actor.

HONG KONG
I have done some temping at a legal firm. And I have a minor in Agrabanian studies. Not to mention serving with distinction as a Pi-con representative in mock Quorum of the Twelve gatherings as part of the Exodus Chronicles Re-enactment Society.

ALI ABABWA
    We'll represent ourselves.

HONG KONG
    No, guys, you don't want to do that –

ALI HAKIM
    Who can speak more eloquently about the
    complicated circumstances of our lives?

HONG KONG
    Me. I can.

ALI HAKIM
    Don't worry, we've seen this movie a dozen times.

ALI ABABWA
    Hear! Hear!

HONG KONG
    You're going to do something weird. It'll make you
    look bad.

ALI ABABWA
    Overruled.

ALI HAKIM
    Yes. Please. I translate loosely from the Agrabanian.
    "You never really understand a person until you
    consider things from his point of view ... until you
    climb into his skin and walk around in it." (*walks
    around as if inside someone else's skin*) Atticus Finch,
    To Kill a Mockingbird.

HONG KONG
    Exactly what I'm talking about. Sorry, ma'am.

SUKI
It's all right. Look, I'm going to do everything in my
power to ensure that you get a fair hearing. That's a
good thing about being in Canada.

ALI ABABWA
Thank you.

SUKI
Okay, so ...

ALI ABABWA
Permission to treat the judge as beautiful.

HONG KONG
Denied.

SUKI
Whoa, whoa, let's have some order here.

HONG KONG
This isn't a game.

ALI ABABWA
But I am under oath. I must tell the truth, the whole –

HONG KONG
Just sit down.

SUKI
Please. Let's just start with some basic details.

ALI HAKIM
Permission to treat the judge as hostile.

HONG KONG
No –

ALI ABABWA
Granted.

SUKI
You currently reside at ...?

ALI ABABWA
(*yelling, accusatory*) Salim's Falafel Shoppe!

ALI HAKIM
(*yelling, accusatory*) In the back!

SUKI
What are you doing?

ALI HAKIM
Treating you as hostile.

ALI ABABWA
There is no law without order!

HONG KONG
They watch a lot of TV.

ALI ABABWA
So many channels. Six for classic movies alone. Five different *CSI*s. Not to mention *World's Biggest Loser*. *Dancing with the Stars. Australia's Next Top Model.* It is how we know so much about your Canadian culture.

SUKI
Okay, so in their own interest, I am going to appoint you as their counsel.

HONG KONG
    Thank you.

ALI ABABWA
    Please, I insist. Hong Kong is no lawyer.

HONG KONG
    Sun Hyung. It's pronounced *Sun* ... *Hyung* – Paul,
    okay? And I'm the best chance you have to deal with
    this mess.

ALI ABABWA
    Madam, Hong Kong is no lawyer, but one of the finest
    yellow actors of his generation.

ALI HAKIM
    We discovered him in children theatre's tour of
    Oh Granny, Why Dat Ackee Fish Gwan So Sad?

ALI ABABWA
    He played a dancing starfruit. He was outstanding.

ALI HAKIM
    Sing her the song!

HONG KONG
    Guys ...

ALI HAKIM
    Sing. I order you.

HONG KONG
    I am not going to sing a song from the kids' show.

ALI ABABWA
    But it goes to the heart of the matter.

ALI HAKIM

It is critical. It expresses the fundamental principle of
modern justice.

SUKI

If it'll make you feel better, I'm happy to permit it.
That's the whole Today's RCMP thing. You know, to
offer flexible processes that can respond to culturally
specific conditions. (*to audience*) Feel free to pass
that along.

HONG KONG

Ma'am, really, it's not – It's a song. From a children's
theatre –

SUKI

Go on. I'm kind of curious.

> *HONG KONG sings and dances.*

HONG KONG
(*singing loudly*)

> Why dat ackee fish gwan so bad
> It so stinky it makee feel sad
> Need a bit o' sunshine makee feel proud
> Need a bit o' jah! Makee shout out loud
>
> If you cut me open you'll see inside ...
> We all be the same no reason to hide

> *ALI ABABWA and ALI HAKIM join on the chorus.*

ALI ABABWA, ALI HAKIM & HONG KONG
(*singing*)

> Iree! Iree!
> We all be the same no reason to hide

SUKI
That was pretty good. But not really relevant.

ALI ABABWA
Cut me open, you'll see inside!

ALI HAKIM
We all be the same no reason to hide. It's Atticus
Finch meets Raffi.

SUKI
Singing notwithstanding, my ruling stands. You're
their representative and cultural translator. Now ...
this place you work – Salim's Falafel Shoppe, it's in
the Market?

ALI ABABWA
Yes, Your Worship.

SUKI
You live there too.

ALI ABABWA
Yes.

SUKI
Sleep in the back. Next to the onion bags.

ALI HAKIM
How do you know that?

SUKI
We know quite a bit about you. Who you see, what
you read. Even what movies you watch. *The Moammar
Gaddafi Story?*

ALI HAKIM

A fine self-portrait by the colonel himself.

SUKI

It was ninety-seven days overdue.

ALI HAKIM

Well, Blockbuster eliminated late fees.

SUKI

According to your computer records, you illegally downloaded *A Few Good Men* 112 times.

ALI ABABWA

A Few Good Men is a great movie.

ALI HAKIM

Jack Nicholson is a very fine actor. The courtroom showdown with Tom Cruise ...?

ALI ABABWA

(*quoting the film*) "Private Santiago was a substandard marine."

HONG KONG

"I want the truth."

ALI ABABWA & ALI HAKIM

"You can't handle the truth!"

SUKI answers her phone.

SUKI

(*on phone*) Brittany? You can't call me now. Oh yeah. He's teething. There should be a teething ring. In the

freezer. It's like a hard rubber ring with little bumps?
Brittany, I have to go. Okay. Bye.

(to ALI ABABWA and ALI HAKIM) Sorry about that.
Child care. Now, tell me about Salim's Friendly
Arabian Falafel Shoppe.

ALI HAKIM
> What would you like to know?

SUKI
> Oh, I don't know. How about *what's on the menu?*

ALI HAKIM
> Falafel?

ALI ABABWA
> We also make excellent shawarma.

SUKI
> How about bubble tea?

ALI ABABWA
> That too.

HONG KONG
> Ma'am, can I ask. What's the relevance of this line of
> questioning?

SUKI
> *(to audience)* Ladies and gentlemen, terrorist
> operatives often use seemingly innocuous words to
> discuss their nefarious acts. Is "bubble tea" some
> kind of code?

ALI ABABWA
Oh sure, it stands for "bomb Toronto."

ALI HAKIM
Oh yes. Every time someone orders a bubble tea, we bomb Toronto.

They ululate and laugh at their hilarious joke.

HONG KONG
They're joking, ma'am.

SUKI
Not very funny.

HONG KONG
Many of their jokes are like that.

SUKI
Is that a cultural thing?

ALI HAKIM
Well, Agrabanians invented irony. Among many other things.

ALI ABABWA
Madam, you have gardened the wrong impersonation. I love this country.

SUKI
Why does Salim use the name Salim when his real name is Firouz Parsa?

ALI ABABWA
It is ...?

ALI HAKIM
    ... his falafel name.

ALI ABABWA
    Falafel name?

SUKI
    Did you know that your friend Salim Falafel also has
    connections to the Al-Jambalayas?

ALI ABABWA, ALI HAKIM & HONG KONG
    Bless you.

SUKI
    A loose network of Montreal-based radicals.

ALI HAKIM
    Radicals? What do you mean by radical?

SUKI
    They are very close to the APF.

ALI HAKIM
    A ... P ... uh ... F?

SUKI
    The Agrabanian People's Front. Don't pretend you
    haven't heard of it. I'd venture to say you've more than
    heard of it. I'd venture to say you're involved.
    Canada's Conservative government considers the APF
    a terrorist organization. It's banned in this country,
    gentlemen, because it is responsible for the cold-
    blooded deaths of civilians across your region.

HONG KONG

That's a fairly sensational description of a very
complex organization, Constable. The APF is not a
monolith. There are a lot of competing interests:
Marxist-Leninist, nationalist, fundamentalist, post-
structuralist, vegetarian. And, what you *really* need to
understand –

SUKI

That's fine. I'm pretty sure it's covered in the dossier.

ALI HAKIM

The Agrabanian People's Front represents the
national and democratic interests of the –

SUKI

So you have heard of the APF, Mr. Hakim.

A silence.

PROJECTION (image)
ALI ABABWA and ALI HAKIM with video cameras
and notepads in front of a nuclear power plant

SUKI

This surveillance photo was taken at a NUC-SEC
Level 3 facility in early January. Mr. Ababwa, can you
tell me what you were doing there?

HONG KONG
Go ahead.

ALI ABABWA
Research.

SUKI

Research at a nuclear facility. What for?

ALI ABABWA

The opening scene: "The Night Everything Changed."

SUKI

Scene?

ALI HAKIM

Yes, you know. From our theatre-play. The one we are
currently not performing.

HONG KONG

It's the first scene in the show. You must have missed it.

SUKI

That South Asian thing? With the puppet?

HONG KONG

Yeah.

SUKI

Oh yeah, I saw it.

HONG KONG

I'm sorry.

ALI ABABWA

It is one of three scenes. They all take place night of
President Osbama's election.

ALI HAKIM

Each one a tribute to the change he has brought to the
lives of everyone across the world. We'll show you the
second scene right now.

ALI ABABWA

(*to HONG KONG*) Fool, set up for Bernie!

SUKI

Are you entering this as evidence?

> *ALI ABABWA and ALI HAKIM exit to change costumes.*

HONG KONG

Yes, Constable. I think we are.

VOICE-OVER

Co-developed for seven years, in collaboration with CEOs Are People Too Society and Puppets for Profit, Ali and Ali are proud to present a demonstration presentation of ...

> *PROJECTION (text)*
> November 4, 2008.
> The Night Everything Changed, Part 2

> *HONG KONG plays JAZZ, the daughter. FLUFFY, BERNIE's wife, is the bunraku puppet in a rich wife outfit, manipulated by ALI ABABWA. JAZZ watches TV. It's U.S. election night. Door. Wind. Door.*

> *Enter ALI HAKIM as BERNIE, brushing snow off his shoulders and clutching a Starbucks mug.*

BERNIE

Crap news. I've been laid off my job as a broker of Debt Default Risk Swaps. Whole firm's gone tits up.

FLUFFY

Shit, Bernie. What are we going to do?

48

BERNIE
Make me some black tea–crusted rack of lamb with
Peruvian mountain potatoes in a villanelle reduction.

FLUFFY
We can't afford the locally sourced truffles.

BERNIE
Fuck me eighteen times, Fluffy.

FLUFFY
I should be so lucky.

BERNIE
I should have used my advanced degree in theoretical
economics to do some good for society, not greedily
enrich us at the expense of millions of people around
the globe.

JAZZ
Dad. Come and watch this.

BERNIE
What is it, Jazzy?

JAZZ
Barack Hoossayn Osbama.

BERNIE
Oh yeah. The Muslim socialist terrorist. (*makes
monkey noises*)

JAZZ
He's a Democrat, Dad.

BERNIE

Exactly what I fucking said.

JAZZ

I think he's going to become president of the United
States.

BERNIE

Yeah, right. And I'm going to become director of
development at the Canadian Atomic Medical Isotope
Institute and save the lives of cancer patients through
my new ethical career.

FLUFFY

Jesus, Bernie! Don't be such a prick.

BERNIE

You're right. I apologize, Jazzy. I'm a fucking asshole.
It's 'cause of the pain I'm feeling about single-handedly
triggering the collapse of the global financial system.
Fluffy, baby. I'm sorry I'm such a loser. You should
have married Moses Znaimer, fucking prick.

FLUFFY

I married you, Bernie, and there's not a goddamn
thing I can do about that. You want one of my
Seconals? Like Grandma Felicity said, "Life's always
better when you can't feel your feet."

JAZZ

The results from Florida are coming in!

They gather around the TV.

BERNIE, FLUFFY & JAZZ
By the holy foreskin of Moses ...

JAZZ
This is a whole new era of hope and change.

BERNIE
I bet he has a really big cock.

JAZZ
Don't you see? *Everything's different now.*

The phone rings.

BERNIE
If that's any boys trying to get into her pants, you tell
them that Jazzy's still in rehab.

FLUFFY
It's for you, Bernie. It's the Canadian Atomic Medical
Isotope Institute. They want you to be their director of
development and save the lives of cancer patients
through your new ethical career.

BERNIE
Oh ... Fluffy.

JAZZ
I love you, Dad.

BERNIE
I love you too, Jazzy.

FLUFFY
Everything really is different now.

Music. Lights. Applause. ALI ABABWA and
ALI HAKIM exit to change.

SUKI

That's even worse than the first scene.

ALI HAKIM

Everybody's a critic.

SUKI

(*to HONG KONG*) You were good, though. Like, I
actually believed you.

HONG KONG

Thanks.

HONG KONG exits quickly to change.

SUKI

Okay, so they went to the nuclear power plant to
research that?

ALI HAKIM

Of course. We are professionals.

HONG KONG

It's true. I went with them. They tried to interview the
core fusion director at Pickering.

ALI ABABWA

You see, your suspicions are baseless, madam.

ALI HAKIM

Perhaps you would like to let the Twitterverse
know that you interrupted our theatre-play for no
good reason.

SUKI

We have reasons. Plenty. Mr. Ababwa and Mr. Hakim
fit a key segment of the profile.

HONG KONG

Profile?

SUKI

Perfect match. In terms of their activities, their
psychology, and so on.

ALI ABABWA

Is this about my mother? Because I've really worked
through a lot of that.

SUKI

Failed and/or frustrated performers. I call it *Canadian
Idol* Syndrome. I wrote a paper on it for the *Alberta
Journal of Alternative Criminology*. On the surface, it
appears counterintuitive. It looks like these people
have bought into the American or Canadian dream.
But – there's a characteristic that predisposes them to
radicalize: sensation seeking. The point for these
people is, to put it in terms you might understand,
the thrill: jihad or *Canadian Idol*. It's all the same.

ALI HAKIM

I'm no expert but they seem quite different to me.

SUKI

It's pretty cutting edge. I've actually been invited to
deliver a keynote in Arizona.

ALI ABABWA

What are we talking about?

SUKI

Just before you entered Canada, you travelled to
Yemen, through the DRC; you were detained in
Axerbijanistan and crossed the Pakistani border.

ALI ABABWA & ALI HAKIM

Yes.

SUKI

So you freely admit to travelling to three fronts on
the war on terror, one after the other, and then coming
to Canada?

ALI ABABWA

We were doing our theatre-play.

ALI HAKIM

It was a great show.

SUKI

Let the record show the Toronto *Star* said:
"Only friends and family would like this show."

HONG KONG

Correction, Your Honour. That was the CBC. The *Star*
said they were like a bunch of "shouting amateurs."

ALI ABABWA

(*shouting*) Shut up, fool.

SUKI

The defendants will stop being mean to their counsel!
God!

HONG KONG

Bad reviews are not exactly grounds for deportation, Constable.

SUKI

Canadian Idol Syndrome. It fits the profile. And you have remained in Canada, illegally, for more than six years.

ALI HAKIM

Promoter assured us everything was on the up and up.

ALI ABABWA

I have made an application for citizenship. I wish to become naturalized Canadian. Like you.

SUKI

I'm not naturalized. I was born here.

ALI ABABWA

Sure, sure.

SUKI

I was. My parents came the hard way. I love them for it. They stood in lines and waited for years. They didn't jump the queue. They came here and they swallowed their pride and their degrees and they worked hard. (*referring to audience*) I bet there's a few stories like that out there right now, gentlemen. And thing is, folks like us, we get a little tired of people like you who stroll into our country and take advantage of the freedoms we fought for.

ALI ABABWA

No, I agree completely. That is why I have engaged
Coco to work for us.

SUKI

Coco? (*she leafs through dossier*) Who's Coco?

HONG KONG

An immigration consultant. I told him half of them
are scam artists.

ALI ABABWA

Coco said in Canada today is dangerous to go through
official channels. He says system is racist, and does
not work for us brown people.

SUKI

That's a good one.

HONG KONG

I told him, it's about being an engineer or computer
programmer, not what colour you are.

ALI ABABWA

Sometimes they steal your kidneys. Coco knows. He
put us on fast track to citizenship. Is very expensive,
but Coco says it is going very well. We are this close ...

ALI HAKIM

Ali Ababwa can be very naive.

ALI ABABWA

No, I have some faith in this country. It is not corrupt
like Agraba, Ali Hakim.

SUKI
What's Coco's last name?

ALI ABABWA
I don't know. I'll check.

SUKI
You don't know his last name?

HONG KONG
Did this Coco have any credentials?

ALI ABABWA
He has a degree from University of Copacabana.

SUKI
Is that why you went to Montreal two summers ago?
To meet this Coco?

ALI ABABWA
Montreal? No, I went for vacation.

SUKI
Vacation?

ALI ABABWA
Is beautiful. You hardly feel like you're in Canada.

SUKI
What was the purpose of your visit?

ALI ABABWA
Ah ... to visit? Agrabanian Centre for Culture and
Taxis also has an office.

SUKI
So does Al-Jambalaya.

ALI ABABWA
Bless you.

SUKI
The radical cell associated with the APF.

ALI ABABWA
If you say so.

SUKI
I do. It's right here in the dossier. And *Canadian Idol* was auditioning that very same week.

ALI ABABWA
I see.

SUKI
Lot of mosques in Montreal.

ALI ABABWA
I guess.

SUKI
You guess.

ALI ABABWA
Yes. I am Christian.

SUKI
Right.

ALI ABABWA
I went to many churches.

SUKI

You're a religious person? Devout?

ALI ABABWA

Not exactly. But they are beautiful buildings. I went to
the big church on the hill they call a mountain. This
church was the sight of many miracles, peoples
healed. Today they still climb the many stairs on hand
and knee. It is so rare to see, here.

SUKI

What?

ALI ABABWA

People who will bow down, who say, "I am not big,
but small, I am not powerful, but powerless." (*silence*)
I have a prayer from church, I wrote down –

SUKI

Just wanting to be Canadian isn't good enough for
citizenship, Mr. Ababwa. You have to believe in this
country. In its values. In the way we do things here.

ALI ABABWA

I do.

SUKI

(*consulting a file and reading*) "May the Blood of the
Infidel Run Thick Through the Streets of Our
Enemies." Is this phrase in any way familiar to you?

ALI HAKIM

Of course. We wrote it.

ALI ABABWA

We are very proud of it.

SUKI

(*to audience*) You hear that, folks? They feel "proud" of having written something called, and let me speak very clearly here, "May the Blood of the Infidel Run Thick Through Streets of Our Enemies."

ALI HAKIM

Of course, it was hugely popular. Quite controversial, but this worked in our favour. It was picked up all across the Middle East.

SUKI

Right. So you freely admit to penning a jihadist tract which calls for the murder of innocent civilians across the West.

ALI ABABWA

Well, I think it's a little more nuanced than that. Shazam Jerkwadi is quite a complex character.

SUKI

Character?

HONG KONG

It was a television series. In Agraba.

PROJECTION (image)
Hideous poster from the TV series

Dramatic music plays.

SUKI
A TV series?

ALI ABABWA
Prime time. Ran for seven seasons. Three Golden Goats.

SUKI
You're telling me that in your country, on network
television, during prime time, children watch this?
This hate-mongering Islamofascist propaganda?

ALI HAKIM
Yes. Is based on U.S. TV show, 24. You know,
Jack Bauer. Every twenty-four hours he must torture
seventeen guys to save the free world. Is great.
We stayed very close to the 24 template.

HONG KONG
I auditioned for it once.

ALI HAKIM
Surely you understand that just because we wrote a
show that celebrates global jihad and beheading
Westerners, it doesn't mean we actually *support* global
jihad and beheading Westerners.

ALI ABABWA
It's just good TV.

SUKI
All right. Tell me about the *Brampton bin Ladens*.

ALI ABABWA, ALI HAKIM & HONG KONG
Ooooo.

ALI ABABWA

They're a family in Brampton who have the
misfortune of sharing a last name with the world's
most notorious terrorist. Multicultural mayhem!

ALI HAKIM

We have many concepts we are developing.

HONG KONG

Somali Pirates of the Caribbean. I love that one!

ALI ABABWA

And not just blockbusters. Also crappy things no one
will watch for CBC.

SUKI

These are all TV shows?

ALI ABABWA

In the development phase, looking for forward-
thinking producers to green light.

ALI HAKIM

Once again, madam, you are confusing cultural
production with real life.

ALI ABABWA

Happens to me all the time. For quite some time I
believe I am father of Justin Bieber.

ALI HAKIM

Is true. Now, madam, surely this travesty of a trial has
gone far enough. (*to audience*) Don't you think so,
good people? Yes, of course you do. The people,
Madam Constable Singh, have spoken, and who are

we to oppose the will of the people? Let us return to our latest award-winning variety show: *Yo Mama, Osbama*, starring Hong Kong Lee!

SUKI
What about *Arms for Agrabanians*?

Silence.

Instruct your clients to answer the question. What is *Arms for Agrabanians*?

ALI HAKIM
I plead the fifth.

ALI ABABWA
Overruled!

HONG KONG
Your Honour, my clients are clearly under duress. If deported, they face arrest and torture. Their homeland is currently under occupation. The elected government is in exile. My clients claim protection under the UN Charter.

SUKI
Canada's Conservative government has instructed us to ignore pleas under the Charter.

ALI HAKIM
I object.

HONG KONG
You're out of order.

ALI HAKIM

I'm out of order? *You're* out of order! This whole
courtroom is out of order!

ALI ABABWA

What is this so-called justice you practise here in
Canada, in which two innocent refugees are
ambushed

ALI HAKIM

by a dissembling harpy

ALI ABABWA

brutally attacked

ALI HAKIM

beaten senseless.

HONG KONG

That's enough!

SUKI

Nobody's been beaten! You've seen me. I've been
more than fair. I asked a very simple question: What
can you tell me about *Arms for Agrabanians?*

ALI HAKIM

You want answers?

SUKI

I want the truth.

ALI HAKIM

You are right, Pivot of the Universe. Answer the
question, Ali!

Dramatic music creeps in. Dramatic lighting.

ALI ABABWA
"Private Santiago was a substandard marine. He was being transferred off the base because –"

HONG KONG
"But that's not what you said. You said he was being transferred because he was in grave danger."

ALI ABABWA
(*pause*) "Yes. That's correct, but –"

HONG KONG
"You said, 'He was in danger.' I said, 'Grave danger.' You said –"

ALI ABABWA
"I know what I said."

SUKI
(*to ALI HAKIM*) Okay, what the heck is going on here?

ALI HAKIM
Shhhh. This is the scene! Classic!

ALI ABABWA
"You snotty little bastard."

HONG KONG
"I'd like an answer to the question, Judge."

ALI HAKIM
"The Court'll wait for an answer."

HONG KONG

"Kendrick ordered the Code Red, didn't he? Because that's what you told Kendrick to do. And when it went bad, you cut these guys loose. You had Markinson sign a phony transfer order. You doctored the log books. I'll ask for the fourth time. You ordered –"

ALI ABABWA

"You want answers?"

HONG KONG

"I think I'm entitled to them."

ALI ABABWA

"You want answers?!"

HONG KONG

"I want the truth."

ALI ABABWA

"You can't handle the truth! Son, we live in a world that has walls. And those walls have to be guarded by men with guns. Who's gonna do it? You? You, Lieutenant Weinberg?"

> *Beat.*

"I have neither the time nor the inclination to explain myself to a man who rises and sleeps under the blanket of the very freedom I provide, then questions the manner in which I provide it."

HONG KONG

(*quietly*) "Did you order the Code Red?"

ALI ABABWA
"I did the job you sent me to do."

HONG KONG
"Did you order the Code Red?"

ALI ABABWA
"You're goddamn right I did!"

ALI HAKIM
AHA! We got the confession! Hong Kong, have this person (*pointing to SUKI*) removed from the courtroom and beheaded!

ALI ABABWA and ALI HAKIM charge SUKI.
Scared, SUKI pulls out her Taser.

ALI ABABWA & ALI HAKIM
(*freeze in mid-charge, then turn and exhort the audience*)
ATTICA! ATTICA! ATTICA!

HONG KONG
(*holding up his iPhone*) Guys, shut up! Constable Dhaliwal, put the Taser away! I am currently recording you on my iPhone!

SUKI
Okay, okay, okay! Let's just everybody take a deep breath.

They all inhale and hold their breath.

SUKI
Are you breathing? Everybody breathe! Calm the hell down. I can't have some kind of incident.

HONG KONG

Of course. We understand. And we want to co-operate.
Don't we? Guys?

ALI ABABWA

Of course.

ALI HAKIM

We are compliance itself.

ALI HAKIM exits.

SUKI

I understand that this is a stressful process. It's
stressful for me too.

ALI ABABWA

Your aura is all jangly.

SUKI

I'm sorry ... about the Taser.

HONG KONG

No harm done.

SUKI

(*very upset*) I feel bad, you know. We're trying to work
toward being more sensitive about different kinds of
people's relationship to this process. I just did a
sensitivity training workshop last week, and what do I
do? I whip out my Taser at the first mention of a
beheading. And I'm actually the head of the diversity
committee. I should know better. I should be setting
an example. I mean, some of my colleagues ...

ALI ABABWA
> You are doing wonderful job under trying
> circumstances.

SUKI
> Truth is, we didn't get a ton of training on this PEIU
> thing. It was rushed in super fast.

ALI ABABWA
> It is the white man's law. Not meant for you and me.

SUKI
> The law is colour blind.

ALI ABABWA
> (*soothing*) Of course it is. Deep breaths. (*quietly*) Is the
> tea ready, Ali Hakim?

ALI HAKIM
> (*off*) Just steeping.

HONG KONG
> I just want to say, I've spent a lot of time with these
> guys. I can say they're good people. Underneath it all.

ALI ABABWA
> We hold you in high esteem too, Hong Kong.

SUKI
> Well, I appreciate you vouching for them but ...

> *ALI HAKIM arrives with tea.*

SUKI
> Thank you.

ALI HAKIM
Sip it very slowly, madam.

She knocks it back.

SUKI
What was that scene you guys were doing?

HONG KONG
The climax. From *A Few Good Men.*

SUKI
I like your acting. (*to HONG KONG*) But you
shouldn't encourage them.

HONG KONG
I get to be Tom Cruise.

SUKI
Yeah.

*While SUKI and HONG KONG are talking,
ALI ABABWA and ALI HAKIM try to sneak away.*

HONG KONG
And I mean, if you think about it, it's kind of relevant.
What Jack Nicholson does to Private Santiago in the
name of freedom is kind of what you're doing here. In
the name of protecting our freedom. I mean, not you,
but the government, or whatever.

ALI HAKIM
Yes, Tom Cruise has much to teach us.

HONG KONG
It's not just Maher Arar. Do you remember the guy
from Ottawa who ended up tortured in Syria 'cause
CSIS found an Ottawa city map in his truck?[4] Or the
men being held under security certificates, or that
other guy – Benatta?[5] Canadian officials drove him
into the States and he was held for five years even
though the FBI cleared him – or like right now, with
the Ottawa Four, there's this hysteria. Like when
Boltar finally realizes –

(to ALI ABABWA and ALI HAKIM) Guys. Come
back here.

> ALI ABABWA and ALI HAKIM have almost made it
> to the exit.

ALI HAKIM
(indicating Exit sign) So CLOSE.

> ALI ABABWA touches the sign wistfully.

SUKI
Is that like Battlestar Galactica?

HONG KONG
You like Battlestar?

SUKI
Gosh, that's good tea. (tries to eat the saucer)

ALI HAKIM
Agrabanian tea.

---

4. Ahmad Abou El Maati.
5. Benamar Benatta, held without charge longer than any other suspect in
   U.S. history.

71

HONG KONG
What I'm trying to say –

ALI HAKIM
It can be quite strong.

HONG KONG
In a climate of fear –

ALI ABABWA
The first time can pack a real punch.

HONG KONG
You say the word "terrorist" –

ALI HAKIM
It's the special herbs and spices.

SUKI sings a Spice Girls song about postracial and intergalactic harmony. ALI ABABWA, ALI HAKIM, and HONG KONG sing backup.

ALI HAKIM
Oh, Bhutto Spice. We're so glad you have come to your senses. Let us get back to the show.

ALI ABABWA
Let's skip to the puppets.

SUKI
Puppets?

ALI ABABWA
Act 4, Scene 6.

SUKI
Is it funny?

ALI HAKIM
Very funny.

SUKI
Your kind of funny, or actually funny?

HONG KONG
Constable, I really need you to hear this. In this
climate of hysteria, when someone gets accused of
being a threat to national security, they instantly
become guilty in the eyes of the public. We start to
believe that it's okay to go to any length to defend
ourselves from threats that – frankly – are way less
likely to happen than almost anything – lightning
strikes, car accidents –

SUKI
I like actually funny. Let's see what you got!

ALI HAKIM
(to HONG KONG) Get over here, fool. You're in
this bit.

   *Intro music. They set up a puppet show with live video
   camera ...*

(to audience) Ladies and gentlemen, we now have the
honour to present to you one of our country's most
beautiful artistic traditions: The Classical Puppet
Theatre of Agraba!

   *"Jungle Boogie" plays. Curtain opens to reveal
   President OSBAMA talking to a CHORUS OF
   BLACK REVOLUTIONARIES who are floating in
   the Oval Office, hovering near the ceiling.*

CHORUS

Shit, Barry. Why you fightin' a war in Afghanistan?

OSBAMA

My name is Barack.

CHORUS

Shut up, mothafucka! You killing our Muslim brothers and sisters.

BIDEN enters.

BIDEN

Who are you talking to, Mr. President?

OSBAMA

My conscience. It's a chorus of African-American revolutionaries.

BIDEN

Do you want me to crush them for you?

OSBAMA

That's okay, Vice-President Biden. They're a minor distraction.

CHORUS

Distraction? We're the voice of the revolution, Uncle Tom fool.

BIDEN

Let's call the meeting to order.

OSBAMA

Joe, the polls show that no matter how reasonably I speak, 50 percent of Americans believe I'm married to Osama bin Laden.

BIDEN

I'm gonna shove those polls up the ass of the pollster who gave them to you!

OSBAMA

Now, now, Joe.

BIDEN

Sorry, son. You're right. You always say: "Highlightify the positive. Disintegrate the negative."

OSBAMA & BIDEN

(singing)

Spew forth the mostly affirmative.
And never say what you really mean.

BIDEN

However, the American public is responding well to your decision to sort of change America at home while continuing to kick the crap out of the rest of the world.

CHORUS

Sheeiitttt! CHANGE! You know what dat stands for? Come help a nigga get elected!

BIDEN

And I do think it was a fantastic idea to change the name of the War on Terror to "Overseas Contingency Operations."

OSBAMA

More syllables can be quite effective.

BIDEN

It's great, nobody cares about it anymore. Sounds
boring.

CHORUS

That's a load a honky-ass establishment bullshit! You
keepin' fifty thousand troops in Iraq! And forty-five
hundred special-ops. You got more drone attacks on
Pakistan dan bullet holes in 2Pac Shakur.

OSBAMA

(*sigh*) Where's Clinton?

BIDEN

Shtupping the Queen of Dubai.

OSBAMA

(*laughs in a friendly way*) No, Joe, I meant Hillary
Clinton, our Secretary of State.

CHORUS

Hillary can handle herself, mothafucka. Why ain't you
putting Bush and Cheney in prison? Those two
crackers make Bashar Al-Assad look like Mother-
Fucking-Teresa. And why you approving a coup in
Honduras? What are you? Some Cold War dinosaur?

OSBAMA

Guys, I understand there's anger out there. I'm angry.

CHORUS

That's pretty funny, boy, 'cause right now you don't look angry – you look like Martin Luther King laid out on a Memphis porch, after he was gunned down by DA MAN!

OSBAMA

You simply don't understand the reality of politics. Compromise. The Art of the Possible.

CHORUS

Fuck tha' reality of politics. Babylon must burn.

BIDEN

I'm going to go get us six cheeseburgers.

OSBAMA

Supersize tha' shit, honky-ass motherfucker.

BIDEN

What?

OSBAMA

Uh, I'll take a McOriental Salad.

Exit BIDEN. Enter BILL CLINTON.

BILL

Sorry I'm late, bro. I was busy bonin' the intern ... uh, I mean saving the Africans.

OSBAMA

Oh hi, Bill.

BILL

You dweebs invite any girls?

OSBAMA

Have you met Stephen Harper?

BILL

Can't say that I have.

OSBAMA

He's here with a tour of the White House.

STEPHEN HARPER enters.

HARPER

Bon jour.

I'm the prime minister of Canada. All of it. Alberta and Quebec and all the other provinces. I shut down Parliament. All the time. Remember the G20? I had helicopters and riot police and everything. That was terrific. I built a lake. It cost a billion dollars.

CHORUS

Sheeeeeit, True North sho ain't what it used to be. Hey, whitey!

They stick a knife in STEPHEN HARPER's head.

HARPER

That feels great.

CHORUS

Shit, he don't die!

HARPER

I won't answer any questions! I'm the prime minister of Canada! On a whole range of issues, my government has taken a very firm position.

BILL

Firm ... position? You wanna see where Monica worked?

HARPER

Sure. Are we going to the Tea Party?

They leave. GEORGE W. BUSH enters in blackface.

G.W. BUSH

Yo, niggaz.

CHORUS

Izzat Dubya? Motherfucker done got hisself an AFRO!

G.W. BUSH

Let's rap, everybody.
(raps)

> Osbama
> yo mama
> you wanna
> with donna
>
> Keeping the White House Black
> mothafucka
> Keeping the White House Black
> mothafucka
> Burning the White House DOWN
> mothafucka mothafucka mothafucka mothafucka
> MOTHAFUCKA!

SUKI

Oh my God! Oh my GOD! That was – You are so
RUDE! OH my God. Mothafucka mothafucka!

ALI ABABWA and ALI HAKIM high-five with SUKI.

SUKI

Oh my God. I don't feel so good. (*exits*)

HONG KONG

(*to audience*) It's the tea. It can be a little harsh coming down.

ALI HAKIM

Ah, Ali Ababwa, bring the hookah. It helps take the edge off. As our prophet Bob Al-Ganouj Al-Marleydin teaches us –

HONG KONG

No! No hookah.

ALI HAKIM

What in your Mongolian upbringing has made you so repressed, Hong Kong?

ALI ABABWA

Did your father not express his affection for you?

SUKI returns.

SUKI

Okay, this hearing is now locked down.

Sirens and flashing lights.

ALI HAKIM

I think the tea has worn off. (*to HONG KONG*) Say something.

HONG KONG

Your Honour, I –

SUKI

No more interruptions. My head is killing me. What
was in that tea?

ALI HAKIM

Herbs and spices?

SUKI

You just attempted to poison an officer of Today's
RCMP.

ALI ABABWA

No, no, madam. Is Agrabanian tea, for relaxing.

ALI HAKIM

Lets your light shine through.

HONG KONG

Constable. Guys, I need you to listen to me. You really
could get deported to Axerbijanistan and you know
what that means. Or they'll stick you in solitary in
Kingston Pen for years. Like the security certificate
detainees.

ALI ABABWA

Who?

HONG KONG

Five guys like you, Muslims –

ALI ABABWA

I'm not a Muslim; I'm a Copt.

HONG KONG

I know.

ALI HAKIM
It's the Christian minority sect of Agraba.

HONG KONG
I know –

ALI ABABWA
(*referring to ALI HAKIM*) *He's* the Muslim. His people have oppressed us since the beginning of time.

HONG KONG
Okay, fine. But they're like you, they're Middle Eastern, Arabs.

ALI HAKIM
I'm not an Arab.

HONG KONG
Whatever! Just listen. The security certificate detainees are JUST LIKE YOU. They were accused of supporting terror. But they never had a trial. There were no charges. And no evidence was ever presented. They were in detention for more than eight years.
(*to SUKI*) Permission to enter photos into the record.

She nods.

PROJECTION (image)
Security certificate detainees

HONG KONG
Mohamed Harkat. Mahmoud Jaballah. Adil Charkaoui. Mohammad Mahjoub. They weren't allowed to touch their kids when they came to visit. Hassan Almrei. He had to go on a hunger strike to get

82

heat in his cell. Mahjoub had to go on a hunger strike
to get treatment for the hep C he got in jail.

Not just them. Maher Arar, everybody knows him. But
what about Muayyed Nureddin, Abdullah Almalki,
Abdelrazik? Their lives turned upside down, denied
the legal rights we take for granted in this country.

It doesn't matter if they have no evidence. Just
accusing you is enough.

A moment.

ALI ABABWA
How is this possible?

SUKI
You want evidence? Tell me about *Arms for
Agrabanians.*

PROJECTION (video clip)
Opening sequence from Arms for Agrabanians *video*

(prerecorded) "Hi, my name is Tom Butler. Though
you may know me better as Captain Sam McKeon
from *Snakes on a Plane* ...

PROJECTION (video clip)
Snakes on a Plane *scene showing Tom Butler as
Captain Sam McKeon*

or Dr. Campbell from *Freddy vs. Jason* ...

PROJECTION (video clip)
Freddy vs. Jason *scene showing Tom Butler as
Dr. Campbell*

... But today I'm not here to entertain you, but rather educate and inform in a fun way.

How many of us have thought about the horrible bloody tragedy unfolding in Agraba and wished there was something we could do? Well, thanks to Ali and Ali, now there is.

PROJECTION (video clip)
Conflict footage. White phosphorus explosions, tanks rolling, troops marching, vehicle convoys, etc.

As you know, decades of war have left many of Agraba's inhabitants permanently maimed. Arms for Agrabanians is a two-pronged initiative designed to make a difference. In part one, Alberta Artificial Limbs Inc. will match every dollar donated tonight by you to be used to purchase prosthetic devices for limbless Agrabanians.

PROJECTION (image)
Prosthetic limbs on display

But of course wars against occupation forces cannot be won with artificial limbs alone. Hence part two, in which Colt Canada makes a similar matching donation toward the purchase of their C7 series of assault rifles and hand-held artillery.

PROJECTION (image)
Shiny new guns

Using their brand new limbs and arms, Agraba's government in exile, the Agrabanian People's Front, will soon be able to mount a credible assault on the imperialist Western forces occupying their homeland.

Limbs and arms. Hand in hand. Thanks to you. I'm
Tom Butler."

Video footage ends.

SUKI
You fundraise for the APF. That's what the video
is for.

ALI ABABWA
We haven't begun this campaign, memsahib. It ... is
just ... an idea.

ALI HAKIM
For a show. Is a joke, madam.

SUKI
Another one of your unfunny jokes. I think most
people would agree that this looks like an attempt to
provide support to a banned terrorist organization. My
only question is whether you are competent enough
to actually do it.

Mr. Hakim, you attend the Al-Jihad mosque, don't you?

ALI HAKIM
Al-Janad. Al-Janad mosque.

SUKI
Pardon me?

ALI HAKIM
There is no Al-Jihad mosque.

SUKI
You heard Nasr Al-Said make a speech there about
global jihad.

ALI HAKIM

Maybe. There are many points of view at the mosque.

SUKI

You were there.

ALI ABABWA

(*to ALI HAKIM*) You went to see Al-Said? But he calls
for the expulsion of Copts from Agraba.

ALI HAKIM

No, his words have been twisted.

ALI ABABWA

He called us cockroaches, Ali Hakim.

A moment.

SUKI

Mr. Ababwa. This money you owe Quickie Cash?
Where did that go?

ALI ABABWA

No, this was for Coco.

SUKI

Your "immigration" consultant.

ALI ABABWA

Yes.

SUKI

Whose last name you don't know.

ALI ABABWA

Well, no.

SUKI
And his office is ...

ALI ABABWA
Well, we meet in the café.

SUKI
In a café? You pay someone how much ...?

ALI ABABWA
Ten thousand dollars.

ALI HAKIM
Ten thousand dollars? Ali Ababwa. Where did ...?

SUKI
I'm going to assume that you don't have any record of
this payment. A cheque stub. Or any way of proving
you didn't give this money to the APF.

ALI HAKIM
Madam, we are proroguing this proceeding!

SUKI
Sit down!

ALI ABABWA
If Stephen Harper can prorogue things, so can we.

We will take our request to the Governor General of
Ali and Ali. An upstanding Canadian citizen of
Mongolian descent. Well qualified to rule on issues of
national consequence.

ALI ABABWA
(to audience) Ladies and gentlemen, we give you
Governor General

ALI ABABWA & ALI HAKIM
    Hong Kong Lee.

    Silence.

ALI HAKIM
    (*running to look backstage*) Hong Kong!

    He's gone.

SUKI
    I guess he had enough.

    A moment.

SUKI
    You give money to the Al-Janad mosque, don't you?
    And that money is funnelled to the Agrabanian
    People's Front.

ALI HAKIM
    …

ALI ABABWA
    Well, sure. We give to mosque just like these people
    give to church –

SUKI
    We? You give to the mosque as well? Why would you,
    Mr. Ababwa, a Coptic Christian, donate money to this
    or any mosque?

ALI ABABWA
    The mosque does much for our community –

ALI HAKIM

We give money to the mosque to support the
Agrabanian People's Front. And I see nothing wrong
with this.

ALI ABABWA

Yes.

SUKI

You acknowledge the mosque is connected to the
Agrabanian People's Front. You acknowledge that you
give money to the Agrabanian People's Front.

ALI ABABWA

The APF is the legitimately elected government of
Agraba.

SUKI

They launch rockets into bordering settlements. They
are dedicated to violent, armed struggle. It's in their
charter. They use human shields. They have little
respect for human life.

ALI ABABWA

I do not always agree with the APF.

SUKI

But you give them money. Why? They persecute
Christians.

ALI ABABWA

Sometimes. It's complicated.

SUKI

They're Islamic fundamentalists.

ALI HAKIM

No, the People's Front is mostly students, Marxists, Jaffarists.

SUKI

Islamists call the shots. Sunni. Or Shia.

ALI HAKIM

Sammi. In Agraba, we are Sammi.

SUKI

What?

ALI ABABWA

Sammi Muslim. They follow a Thirteenth Imam whom they believe assumed the form of a dynamic, one-eyed, African-American, Jewish entertainer named Sammy. Davis Jr.

ALI HAKIM

Not so long ago, the West says Agraba must have election. This will bring peace to our region. We have election. And the APF wins. Now the West says no, this is not acceptable, the APF must go. So they cut off aid, and it is all the people who suffer. So today, even Copts support the Agrabanian People's Front because we do not see why the West should decide what is legitimate or not for Agraba.

ALI ABABWA

The situation in Agraba is complex, madam.

SUKI

Terror isn't complex. Blowing up innocent people. That's simple.

ALI HAKIM
And a drone attack on civilians is complex?

ALI ABABWA
Alexander the Great captured a pirate and angrily
demanded of him, "How dare you molest the seas?"
To which the pirate replied, "How dare you molest the
whole world? Because I do it with a little ship only, I
am called a thief. You, doing it with a great navy
molest the world, and are called an Emperor."[6]

ALI HAKIM
The ANC was once labelled a terrorist organization.
Nelson Mandela was called a terrorist.

SUKI
Nelson Mandela was a respected world leader.

ALI HAKIM
Exactly.

SUKI
I think this country has a reasonable interest in
ensuring that money raised here in Canada does not go
to buy weapons which are then used to kill Canadian
TROOPS! Corporal Janet Ross. She was killed two days
ago by a roadside bomb. She was twenty-one.

ALI ABABWA
Omar Khadr was sixteen when he was taken to
Guantanamo.

SUKI
Do you know the Khadrs?

6. St. Augustine, *City of God*, Book 4, Chapter 4.

ALI ABABWA

No. Do you know Ravi Shankar? How about Yehudi
Menuhin?

ALI HAKIM

May I show you a picture?

SUKI

Is it relevant?

ALI HAKIM

I think so.

*He hands SUKI a wallet-sized photo, the kind
grandmothers carry in their purses. SUKI studies
the picture but says nothing.*

ALI HAKIM

My daughter. She is seven years old next month.

SUKI

She has a lovely smile.

She tries to hand the picture back.

ALI HAKIM

I have never seen her. I have only some photographs
that Ana was able to send me through a friend of a
friend at the mosque. When the war broke out again
in Agraba, we were separated, Ana and I, and the
smuggler who was to take Ana to safety across the
mountains, led her instead straight to detention
centre. Ana was pregnant and Souad was born in
refugee camp. She lived in a plastic tent for the first
two years of her life. I am stateless and wandering,
unable to do anything for my daughter or wife. They

have very poor food, no shoes. Souad loses hearing in one ear from infection. There is no medicine. She cries all the time from pain. Then one day, word comes everyone is to be moved from camp. Ana believes this is a trap, that they are being expelled and left to die. But no. Trucks bring four hundred refugees to new village. New houses. Made of brick. Not plastic. When they arrive, they are given new clothes. Shoes. Food. They visit doctor who gives Souad antibiotics for infection. She stops crying. Ana wrote that at first she thought they had died and gone to Piña Majorca. There is a playground for children. This is where photo is taken. You see? Soon, she will go to new school in village.

Do you know, Constable, who has done all this? Saved my wife and daughter? Built village with doctor, playground, and school? Munificent NGO of the West? No. It is Agrabanian People's Front. Yes, this "terrorist" organization. They have saved the lives of people I love above all others. For them, I am prepared to do anything, Constable. Wouldn't you do the same?

SUKI gives ALI HAKIM the photo back.

SUKI
Yes.

SUKI's phone vibrates. She looks at it. Doesn't answer.

Messieurs Ababwa and Hakim, given the nature of the testimony provided today and the potential danger you pose to the Canadian public, this PEIU court orders your immediate deportation.

A silence.

ALI ABABWA

Very well. We will go to Axerbijanistan, Ali Hakim.
Perhaps we will –

HONG KONG enters.

HONG KONG

Wait. There is a lien against Ali Ababwa. With
accumulated interest, he owes Quickie Cash Payday
Loan Service over twenty-three thousand dollars.

SUKI

Yes and ...?

ALI HAKIM

Twenty-three thousand dollars? By Sammi, Ali
Ababwa!

SUKI

I fail to see the relevance of this.

HONG KONG

He can't be deported! The lien against his assets and
person overrides any legal proceedings. He has to stay
here to pay back the money he owes.

*ALI ABABWA and HONG KONG hug and cheer.
ALI ABABWA rushes to hug ALI HAKIM.*

ALI HAKIM

Your wish has come true, Ali Ababwa. You can stay in
Canada.

ALI ABABWA tries to decide.

ALI ABABWA

I don't want to stay, Constable. Take me to
Axerbijanistan, with my friend, Ali Hakim. I throw
myself on your mercy.

SUKI

Your lawyer is quite right. The debt obligation
supersedes the Immigration Act. I will pass your file
to Financial Enforcement, which I believe is under the
jurisdiction of Transport Canada. One of their officers
will be in touch shortly.

HONG KONG

I couldn't think of anything for you. I knew about his
loan and – I'm sorry.

HONG KONG hugs ALI HAKIM.

ALI HAKIM

No, you did good, Hong Kong. Look after Ali Ababwa.

SUKI

The PEIU proceeding provides an opportunity for
final personal statements. If you would like to say
anything to be entered into the official record, this is
the moment to do so.

HONG KONG

Please, Constable. There's a misunderstanding. I'm
telling you, they're good people. Despite what they
may – or may not – have done ... you have an
opportunity here to show some mercy ... or justice.

SUKI

Mr. Ababwa? (*silence*) Mr. Hakim?

ALI HAKIM

Read me that prayer you carry around, Ali Ababwa.
Brother André.[7] From the church in Montreal.

ALI ABABWA uncrumples a piece of paper and reads.

ALI ABABWA

(*reading*) "Open our compassionate hands in times
of war. Keep us from developing a victim's mentality
and make our pain a source of growth. Refuse
vengeance. Close all doors to bitterness so that we
may dance for joy."

*ALI ABABWA folds it and puts it away – or gives it to
ALI HAKIM.*

ALI HAKIM

Thank you. Goodbye, my friend.

ALI ABABWA

I'll see you. Soon. At Habibi's in Agraba City.

ALI ABABWA hugs ALI HAKIM.

ALI ABABWA & ALI HAKIM
(*singing*)

> Agraba, oh Agraba, long live the green and chrome
> Till we get to Piña Majorca, our one and only home.

*ALI ABABWA and ALI HAKIM make the
Piña Majorca gesture.*

---

7. Brother André (Alfred Bessette) was canonized in Rome on the day we
closed in Toronto. We like to think our theatre-play had something to do
with this recognition. It's not true of course but we like to think it. Brother
André founded St. Joseph's Oratory in Montreal.

ALI ABABWA & ALI HAKIM
May we all find ourselves in Piña.

SUKI handcuffs ALI HAKIM.

SUKI
Let's go.

ALI HAKIM
Allah O Akbar.

SUKI
(*to audience*) Ladies and gentlemen, I apologize once
again for the disruption. You may apply to the Ministry
for compensation for up to (*checks her manual*)
75 percent of the expenses you incurred this evening.
Thanks for your patience. Good night.

She leads ALI HAKIM away.

ALI ABABWA and HONG KONG watch him go.
The lights fade on them slowly.

Suddenly, the sounds of struggle from offstage. Shouts,
banging, Ululation. A Taser is discharged. A scream.
ALI HAKIM runs on, shirtless.

ALI HAKIM
Ali Ababwa!

ALI ABABWA
Ali Hakim?

ALI HAKIM tosses ALI ABABWA an AK-47.

ALI HAKIM
    Hong Kong!

        ALI HAKIM tosses HONG KONG a plastic scimitar.

ALI HAKIM
    Cover me while I roll! (*does a sort of barrel roll thing*)
    Get the chopper.

        *ALI ABABWA, ALI HAKIM, and HONG KONG
        run off.*

SUKI
    WAIT!

        SUKI crawls on.

HONG KONG
    Go. Get to the chopper! I'll hold her off.

        ALI ABABWA and ALI HAKIM run off.

SUKI
    When Ali Hakim Tasered me, something happened. The
    doors of perception are opening. I see you, Hong Kong.

HONG KONG
    I see you too. Constable.

SUKI
    Take me away, Hong Kong. Take me to Timbuktu, to
    drink the sacred yak milk of your ancestors ...

HONG KONG
    I'm from Ottawa.

SUKI
  Shhhhhh.

  *She kisses him under a spotlight as sparkling confetti
  showers down on them.*

  *ALI ABABWA and ALI HAKIM return in new
  orange jumpsuits.*

ALI HAKIM
  (*to audience*) You see, ladies and gentlemen, things
  really are different now.

ALI ABABWA
  It's a whole new era in the world. Once again.

  They dance the Jai Ho routine from the end of
  Slumdog Millionaire.

  END

Acknowledgements

The authors especially thank:
- Amanda Fritzlan; Zak, Oscar, and George Youssef; Tamsin Kelsey; Lorena Dexter Chaichian
- The Cultch, the Canada Council for the Arts, the B.C. Arts Council
- Tom Butler and Paul Sun Hyung Lee for sandwiches and helpful script suggestions

Camyar Chai

Camyar Chai has worked in theatre, opera, film, television, and radio for more than two decades. As a writer, his work ranges from the co-creation of the political satire *The Adventures of Ali and Ali and the aXes of Evil* (published by Talonbooks), to writing the historical musical *Asylum of the Universe* (published by *Canadian Theatre Review*). He has also written librettos for children's opera such as *Elijah's Kite* (Tapestry New Opera / Manhattan School of Music), which received a command performance for the Governor General of Canada. Chai's directing credits include the site-specific production *Bollywood Wedding* (South Asian Arts); *Adrift on the Nile* (Neworld Theatre), a Rio Tinto Alcan Award recipient; and *Mother Courage and Her Children*, which was presented as his University of British Columbia master of fine arts thesis. He is founding artistic director of Neworld Theatre and currently serves as arts coordinator for the City of Richmond, British Columbia. He continues to work as a freelance film and theatre artist, arts mentor, and facilitator.

Guillermo Verdecchia

Guillermo Verdecchia is a writer of drama, fiction, and film;
a director, dramaturge, actor, and translator whose work
has been seen and heard on stages, screens, and radios
across the country and around the globe. Currently, a resi-
dent artist at Soulpepper Theatre in Toronto, where he
heads New Play Development, he is a recipient of the
Governor General's Award for Drama, a four-time winner
of the Floyd S. Chalmers Canadian Play Award, and a
recipient of Dora and Jessie Awards, as well as sundry film
festival awards for his film *Crucero / Crossroads*, based on
his play *Fronteras Americanas* and made with Ramiro
Puerta. He holds a master of fine arts in drama from the
University of Guelph and teaches playwriting at the University of Toronto and at the Soulpepper Academy. He lives
in Toronto with his partner, Tamsin Kelsey, and their two
children, Anaïs and Theo.

Marcus Youssef

Marcus Youssef is artistic director of Vancouver's Neworld Theatre. His plays, many of which were written and/or created with friends and colleagues, have been presented at theatres and festivals across North America, Australia, and Europe. They have received the Rio Tinto Alcan Performing Arts Award, the Floyd S. Chalmers Canadian Play Award, and the Seattle Times Footlight Award, as well as multiple Jessie Awards. Youssef is a graduate of the National Theatre School (Acting), holds a master of fine arts from the University of British Columbia, and teaches widely. He is currently co-chair of the City of Vancouver Arts and Culture Policy Council and sits on the advisory board of the *Canadian Theatre Review*. Youssef lives in East Vancouver with his partner, Amanda Fritzlan, and their sons, Zak and Oscar.